APPEARING SOON

For my family and friends

'In frenetic quest for the unexpected, we end by finding only the unexpectedness we have planned for ourselves. We meet ourselves coming back.'
    (Daniel Boorstin, *The Image*)

APPEARING SOON

Amanda White

Acknowledgements

Some poems in this collection have previously appeared in:
Ambit, *Envoi*, *The Interpreter's House*, *Mslexia*,
New Writing, *Oxford Poetry*, *Pitch* and *Staple*;
and some were published in a leaflet and on the web
for Cornwall Open Studio 2002.
'Bench' was highly commended in the Blue Nose Poets 2000
Lost London: The Millennial Poetry Competition and published
in an accompanying anthology. 'Crabbing at Mersea Island'
was shortlisted in the Bedford Open Poetry Competition 2003.
Some of these poems were first read at Lauderdale
House, Highgate; The Troubadour, Earls Court; Colpitt's,
Durham; and the Ledbury Poetry Festival 2003.

First published in the UK in 2005 by Flambard Press
Stable Cottage, East Fourstones, Hexham NE47 5DX

Typeset by BookType
Cover design by Gainford Design Associates
Author photograph by Andrew Gillman
Printed in England by Cromwell Press, Trowbridge

Copyright © Amanda White 2005

A CIP catalogue record for this book
is available from the British Library.
ISBN 1 873226 71 3

All rights reserved

Flambard Press wishes to thank Arts Council England
for its financial support.

website: www.flambardpress.co.uk

Contents

Appearing Soon	7
Crabbing at Mersea Island	8
Dakota	10
. . . they wait for snow all year, then . . .	13
Bedside Cabinet Drawer: Contents (and Conclusion)	14
A Warm Front	16
A Case of Mistaken Identity	17
Glass Bottomed Boat	18
Dead Bee	19
Stole	20
Animal, Vegetable or Mineral?	22
Diary Entry: Trebah Gardens, Helford River, Cornwall	24
Duplication	25
Kidnap	26
The Way It Goes: Mother/Daughter	28
Evensong	29
Notes on Mapreading	32
Glass Blower	33
Sitter	35
Remembering Songs (Instrumental)	36
The Pictorial Encyclopaedia of Fishes	39
Mine	40
Long Rock	41
Stitchery	42
Bench	43
Shine	45
Stones at Dunster	47
Myrrh	48
The Founded Heart	49
Explaining Mary	50
Holiday Romance: A True Story	51

Bridge/Water	53
Graded Pieces	54
Picnic	55
Scenes in an Afternoon	56
Pin	57
Half an Hour	58
Two Weeks	59
Gatherers	60
Kissing Gourami	61
Hedgerow	62
Lobby	63

Appearing Soon

Sunday walking, only, but there is something more serious
in the foreground always too close to focus on, perhaps the
whirlings of dust, the blurrings of tendrils, cells copulating.
There is only the turning, while they find the openings and
conceal their hurtings. They move on down the tracks that
bear arrows to show them the way even though lost friends
are at their heels, rows of hang-dog elms, observing without
interest, too tired for human bother. Skins. Pelts. They are
see-through, pocketing silences, wanting to forgive and
forget but still holding on to personal grievances. It is best
not to go too far, to settle for a before-lunch or after-lunch
walk, or if for the whole day make sure to pack food and drink.
Careful! There is poison in everything. Buds. Seeds. Leaves.
Rinses of sap. The soft landscape can turn on you just like that.
And when it rains, it will be a steady shower, making a point,
digging at their backs, singling them out, the unprepared
drowned loons falling from themselves into vapour. No
witnesses. Every fern keeping its tight little mouth shut.
But instead of murder they find a rainbow, so close it touches
them, the power of the colours, the simple pleasure of
seeing red and violet as they are meant to be and they
stop in all ways, take it in, remember they are together, still.

Crabbing at Mersea Island

'I get the urge for going
But I never seem to go'
    (Joni Mitchell, *'Urge for Going'*, 1966)

These wetlands, these undreamed, damp stretches, wash up
slack waves tired of their own confined action, working
over the same-old-same-old and as he drives he tells them
how he could have been an Olympic skier or this or that
not the tat and spit that he is juddering about the alcoves
of the world selling plastic tubing. His boys incline over
computer-generated life, murdering while sensing a shift
from mainland to island. His wife, who has prepared for
everything, fixes on a point of never-ending space she knows
must be there beyond a dirty dressing of low huddling clouds.

At the tatty but well reviewed café he orders the shellfish
extravaganza to show the others – trippers, locals, mutant
weekenders – that his children have acquired a taste
and technique that will, with the expert dismembering,
plucking and swallowing, seal their undoubted golden future.
He flashes his choice of bring-your-own, a 1994 Fleurie,
with a shaky flourish to the cans and screw-tops. His family
tighten, a well-practised gut string trying to tune him in.
Glass after glass sinks him. Today he will not bother
to phone her or pretend to have to go into work. Evaporating.

He is desperate to get away from people he never imagined.
They troop down to a crowded pontoon through boats
collared by mud, unbalanced in themselves. Drinking
from the bottle now, he shows off his special rods,
weighted and baited with succulent rashers of streaky bacon.
She attends, zips coats, stops them falling. He tells them
how to reel, count, wait, WAIT, a champion fisherman
himself once, at county level, casting for salmon, walking
on water. *Everyone is looking at you Dad*. His eldest gives
up the rod, no turning back, goes with Mum to solid land.

His youngest stays, anchors him. On a roll, they pull crab after
crab and the man's moment comes, the biggest yet, until in
slow-mo the bastard unhooks, pincer by pincer, before they can
get the net under. They spill the rest to race the slipway.
Back in the car-park she smiles, hands him a Magnum
which he throws down. *I wanted a cornet.* At last she bites,
he knew she would, leaves him kicking up the gravel.
In the background a mirror dinghy arcs a course to open sea.
They go back the way they came. This time he is the one
watching the sky. It comes on to rain, drowning them all.

Dakota

She did not often hear
but missed him more than summer sun
and many a time
swore she saw him coming back
through a fractured mist
carried on its seemingly soft, cradling arms
drenched to the bone
head smashed in
a wrangle of gold knotted to his palm
as he reached out to her,
his Queen, Sweet Betty Sweet,
tendering an uneven smile.

> *Mokelumne Hill, Deer Creek, Yellow Jacket*
> *My rolling home, my rolling heart.*

When he did come back
across the Atlantic to Morvah's white downs
he set straight to building
a house called Dakota
from the spoils of his labours.

> *Camped with the Sioux near Wind Cave,*
> *Slept like a babe beneath a buffalo skin.*

His Dakota was a deep, dark granite place
the bad bone of a badland namesake
not the fresh face of hope he had wished for.
He forgot about the need for bigger windows
wanted to keep the cold out.
No gold specks here just damp skies filed down low
over a land worked by wind and smacked hard back
where the old, dead mines,
like mantraps, gave the finger.

Spearfish, Chollar Potosi, Sylvan Lake,
Near lost an eye from a brawler in Rapid City.

The meagre conspiracy of trees on the back boundary
curved in upon themselves
from the slew of skanky weather
forcing a line, the truth to come out,
old friends near enough all gone
to mine in better places
just a few strays left to drink
and blather out their days
remembering the good times.

Chasing fortune from prairie to canyon,
Bad days a-going, good days a-coming.

She set hard to making sure
he never wanted for anything.
Stilled and held him.
But for all the comfort of a home
and a first love's willing kisses
he found it hard to warm his bones
by his own fire
enough to stay.

Carson City, Charlotte, Philadelphia,
Them that not dead now stay lucky.

When he heard hot talk about Nova Scotia
he drank up the promise of a rich seam
took off that very night,
slid cleanly out from their bed
while she was still sleeping,
away from all that he had once known
and known again,
fast away,

passed the church that had christened and married him,
disappearing into an over-spilling sky
of dead-eyed, flinty stars and a slant, thin moon
glad to have him back.

> *Such vast skies as these I have never seen*
> *Without you they are my dearest comfort.*

Where his last shadow fell
she spat and took herself to heart
a long time coming home
too quick to walk out
the back way across the field
called *Aragabmus* from its crooked shape.

A quiet anger whelked to her swelling gut
where a baby kicked and dug deep,
it did not have a name then
but she would make sure it was soon fixed.

. . . they wait for snow all year, then . . .

Falling
Catching itself out
Conjured by its absence

<u>Embroidered plainly together</u>
The angry yet unspoken thoughts
Spark to a nothing or everything
As shot sun hits a field of fresh snow

Unmarked
Not yet touched by anyone or anything
A stray pine needle cannot help
But want to spoil such a moment.

Bedside Cabinet Drawer
Contents (and Conclusion)

Today, it is reported, was the hottest for half a
century. Every window in the house is open,
tight-lipped and struck dumb. The gloop and glub
of air is swollen with its own importance and pockets
our cross exchange, sends us skittering apart, you to the
crash-landing of sofa to daddy the remote, still your
furious bones, while I exit with loud tears and murder
each stair, stamping out all the moments that have
gone before, arriving to the deliberate slap-across-the-
cheek slam of our bedroom door. I slouch, damp,

hurt and hurting on the edge of the B&B Italia bed we
had saved two years to buy, sheets tangling the
sleekness of its acclaimed and experienced beauty
and line. A belligerent sun seeks me out through the
flit-flap of cheap venetian blinds we fiddled and cut
to fit, doubting our choice as we wasted a weekend.
A soundtrack of suspense tails off, traffic queuing and
leaving the city with murmurs and jolts of siren. He
has not come to me. An angry limbo finds me
making busy, sorting through the bedside cabinet

drawer, a job I had always meant to do like putting
the photographs in albums, learning how to send text
messages, reading *Beloved* again. Laid out: Home
video, me thin and silly at just twenty. A sixty-watt
spare bulb, its partner already gone. A Russian red
watch we bought in Berlin just after the Wall came
down, hands stuck at a never-never time. Silver
Mag-lite torch from your Mum last Christmas, a
stocking filler she had bought for all her boys. Old
keys, near blunted, each blackened and blind finger

having nowhere to poke home. I throw out a rogue
nurofen yellow dot, tears drying on my face, the
argument still burning in my chest. I lay one blue and
one black bic biro parallel, almost touching. Angular
violin rest like a dismembered limb or sculpture or
both. Recent birthday card, orange flower with a red
centre, from him, *Love you forever* written inside. I
keep it. Empty ring case, its pierced and fattened
velvet heart stabbed with a straight, unsmiling
mouth. A white pebble with a crescent hole, chalky

and smooth at the same time, I remember you putting
it in my hands as you pulled me down and kissed me
on the beach at Birling Gap. Still, no sound from
downstairs. I throw away a 'Limes A Ongles' nail file
from the Meridien Hotel where we spent our
wedding night and an old *Telegraph* with the only clue
filled in on the Prize Puzzle, No 1994, ON THE DOT, 3
down: 'He'd not contrived to get up at the right time'
(2,3,3). The unidentifiable relics of dust, hair and time-
made specks are all that is left in the drawer. The

exhibits on the bed seem to offer other stories and I
can see how it is easy to slip, from the evidence, from
love to hate and back again, each interpretation
already jostling for position. The sun finally gives
out, goes down behind the other homes across the
road and leaves me alone. I scoop everything up and
throw them back into the drawer and put myself
away again, button up the spine, wipe down the eyes
and slope back downstairs and slip in beside you and
pick up the tea, still warm, that you had made for me.

A Warm Front

The underdone eyes
That hair
And all behind the day
Fledgling desires
Trailing the air
To smack us raw.
The weather has cleared enough for us to happen.
All this in an afternoon's small talk
Grinning and gripping us tight
on the backs of sun-loungers
(£3 for the day from the ex-windsurfer who rode
a bad double header and has retired at twenty)
We skim each other
The sisters in law
Rehearsing . . . nothing
At times like these it comes down to
No more than bikinis and shoes
On a scale of cheap
And as our husbands play frisbee with the children
We dissolve
Glad for the excuse of heat.
The edge of the world is just over there
By the perfect family playing cricket on the beach
Well lit with the fat lick of late sun
As a high hit ball leaves us looking on blind.

A Case of Mistaken Identity

I love my frozen baby girl
I dress her up sometimes
smelt her eyes open
while her friends are playing elsewhere
bouncing on beds in upstairs houses
as she lies unprincessed in the ground
dreaming of being excited
in huge shoes like unclimbed mountains.

Glass Bottomed Boat

You want me, I can always tell, but I'm down here,
the Blue Damsel fish, forced out by day chewing on a
life form you might take for food. Your stung, familiar
gaze bores me. With the glass window between us
there is no touching and only looking if I let you.

There you are drumming your fingers on the side,
those clumsy, dry pokers you find so hard to keep to
yourself. You are the kind that mistake everything,
the way I am swimming as flirting and when I breathe
you imagine I am licking my lips, coming on to you.

We make eye contact, just before I am eclipsed by
a shoal of dazzlers, cheap parrot fish, and be sure I
know the real reason you came. You had nothing
better to do, lured in by a quick ride around the bay,
having exhausted the beach, the hotel and your own

company. So when I go off into a personal shadow,
tell yourself it's all teasing if that makes you feel
better and tonight you will sink into your own
darkness; a bar, a club, appear to be floating,
just a holiday romance, easy smiles that will get

you close enough so there will be nothing between
you to stop you wanting to smack her around a bit.
She will spend the rest of the night washing you off
and tomorrow you will choose another activity, hire a
jeep, go up into the mountains for some more

sightseeing. I'm waiting here of course for
something else, sex and death in one bite, a big
fucker, a hammerhead to go out on, not years of tank
life, being fed stale scales of myself. I might well
be a different species, but it takes one to know one.

Dead Bee

'There was the hum of bees, and the musky odor of pinks filled the air.'
(Last line from Kate Chopin's The Awakening)

The visitors are late
the house gleams in its own way
I remember somewhere I forgot to put myself in focus
lost on a landing
dusting
evolving to a hot blur of smoothness.
It amuses me to leave a dead bee on the window sill in the kitchen
poised between garden and the inside home it came to
perhaps by mistake or intuition.
It has to be sad of course and too perfect
from the teasing mid-flight stillness of its wings to its inert sting
against my own slow siss of being
acute from waiting for the people to arrive wondering if,
as they ascend the path,
I will find them as I knew them and remember we are friends.
I toy with dismembering the bee's dear dear wings
a queen I am sure
while the survivors are left careering around the garden
nosing into flowers
intoxicated with their own place in the world
ignoring the arrival of my guests
noisy and apparent and meaningful against floods of colour
and an afternoon thrilled with itself just for being hot.
I take myself by my bones up to the front door
hold it ajar
stand in its delicate vice
waiting to see if they will be cut to ribbons
as they come inside.

Bee-keepers are renowned for living longer than most people.

Stole

Further details hide inside the second skin of sapped
and cracked tissue where I keep Auntie Tilly's fox fur
stole almost alive, forgotten mostly but not thrown out.
It lies legless and unworn in the shadows beneath the
future she died before: a cold beaded fuchsia halter-neck
and shower-proof mac that tries to hold me close. It lies
curled in upon itself with the specks and flaws of a past
she ran south from, widowed at fifty, to live alone near
my granny, her elder sister Kath, who was left their
mother's golden marmoset jacket and murdered it for a

quick sale to be cut into trims and cuffs. She kept winter
going well into spring when she came for Sunday roasts
and wore the fox head with its sad but steady glare firm
on her buttoned-down chest, its throat neat sliced for the
loop of tail, her own face set cross, dried blood lips all
scrim and scraw. They said you did not like children but
when I came to visit you after school in warmer weather
and if the mood took hold you might give me iced
fancies with a wink and sit me on your soft pelted lap to
read *Swallows and Amazons*. Once you took foxy

out from his hibernating rest to play dress-up and I
buried my face into its heartless body and threw it
round my shoulders all swank and swagger, dancing
around your lounge before you reined me down to sit at
your feet, telling me not to be too wild while stroking
my hair gently. It was years later before we found her,
perhaps I had glimpsed her in the wet film of your eyes
when you used to say, *cheerio love*, but when I came with
my mother to clear up there she lay, in a tiny field of
maroon velvet, a still shining wheat-yellow baby curl,

inside the old *Frederick's of Sheffield* jewellery case that had once held the weight of a gold watch and chain, and tucked into the lid her folded remains, birth and death certificates for Emily Grace who had lived just three months. I think of the fox sleeping now, at peace from the hounds and the passionless business of the taxidermist's hands, remembering how the stole felt soft when the weather was mild but mostly coarse and matted, smelling sour from all the places and people who had nudged close to Auntie Tilly without really touching.

.mal, Vegetable or Mineral?

'How hard it is to tell what it is like,
this wood of wilderness, savage and stubborn'
          (Dante, *The Divine Comedy, Vol I: Inferno*, Canto I, lines 4 and 5)

alive	yes	She chooses a morning, unsure of the month, to leave behind forty-five years of marriage and a house too clean
vertebrate	yes	its bones poke through the shoals of ornaments, forever tended. Shutting the front door for the last time, the walls
claws	no	catch the coda draught, a warble that wants to become a song that has been written for moments like this and she
pterodactyl	yes	tries to remember the way it goes, certain she will not turn to stone, less certain as to what she has left behind, a brief
tiger	no	doubt, like sheep bones that seem human, better the devil you know . . . passed the prunings, dead headings, happier
dung beetle	no	days gardening together, Nice Mr Dog and Merry Mummy Bear, after a settled spring when the fruit bowl overflowed
dead	yes	with visits from the children and their children filling the difficult turns on the stairs, the quiet nights finding voices
red	no	from the television, with easy laughter and company. It is hard to keep on walking down a path that never seemed
potato	yes	so long She steadies herself, kept going by one too many dinners left waiting to be heated up, the last bruise on her
tomato	yes	arm, the hit he called a push, his bite worse than . . . that photograph, a baby who came in a Christmas card once-upon
pips	no	'with fondest memories' written on the back. His husband faces lie in the variable clouds gathering: charming but
round	no	predatory at parties, sneering behind colleagues' backs, loving oh certainly there had been times between the other
sour	yes	times left waiting all night for him to burn back and hold her, if her had only . . . She did say 'I do', once, more than a
sweet	yes	whisper, blur of lips beneath a frosted veil, itching to be kissed, then, at that moment so sure. Down the avenue,
stone	no	her life clutched close, reduced into a case on wheels, flanked by birch trees determined to cling to their shimmering leaves

stone	yes	and memories – silverscreen, *From Here to Eternity*, once Deborah Kerr to his Burt Lancaster or in that slide on
copper	no	Weston sands paddling gaily but shyly in long, slack waves, a hint of Liz Taylor in *Cleopatra*, only at the time she felt
alive	no	too ugly to believe she had a best side. Ahead, a space in the sky, a slither of semi-precious sunlight, chrysoprase.
poisonous	yes	The bus is molten through hot tears. She melts down to a window seat at the back. Heart beat acute as the door opens
fire	yes	for her usual stop at the shops, haddock on Fridays, and she stays put, worries she has left him enough to see him through.

'Chrysoprase: A very subtle quartz, this 'Joy Stone' helps to ease sexual frustration and depressions by balancing neurotic patterns and by enhancing personal insight.'
(Crystal Health and Wealth, The Efficacious Use of Gems and Minerals)

Diary Entry
Trebah Gardens, Helford River, Cornwall

The unsailed boat is where we land
falling from extravagant palms
finding children in our hand.

Duplication

The mood of the machine takes him down,
its sorter angles a feigned disinterest
but he knows it was well before lunch-time
apologises for the bleeding,
the over-spill of text splintering off the sharp edge.
Every new customer might be an account or a bad word.
He worries about his daughter's eczema.
The shop has so much work on
and the heat from the machines takes him back
from High Holborn to Sri Lanka.
At the end of every day he forces his hands to be clean.
No marks. No marks.
In order, the VAT, hole-punched pages set square
in the grip of a lever-arch file.
Later, his wife's plain bound spine curled shut,
opportunities keeping watch through the bedroom window,
inky shadows tricking themselves they are more than darkness.
He knows she will be scratching in her sleep.
He tracks a plane's slanting lights,
fills in the gaps,
maybes, whys, looking for the perfect copy of himself,
his family, his house, his life and no-one else's,
in black and white,
just once,
A4,
enough.

Kidnap

This autumn the leaves are ransom notes
discarded on the lawn or it may be a field.
Sometimes I am blindfolded and against my will
I can say I do things, unspeakable things,
that I only hope are forgotten by walls and doors
and more doors and fastenings and mortise locks.
It has been a long time I know that much
and my gaoler(s)
(perhaps they are many)
are now people I love and trust.
I am unsure about the exact story I shall tell
when I get out, if and when and if again,
yet on good days I remain acute to details,
shadows that tip and fall over slate sills
and seem to make sense,
a cold tap that reminds me who I might be
when I turn it on and off,
a wind that gets up
across the garden or yard
and knows everything,
laundry and soaps and hair and fingernails,
a sky married to the land at unnerving angles
through the windows and the bars
and an open gate,
being alone but watched,
talking, chatting and not remembering,
kissing, fucking and not kissing just fucking,
being taken out under a coat,
having other people come round
and calling him mostly 'Baby'.
Only I cannot really tell the difference anymore
between torture and not-torture
it just hurts more sometimes
not necessarily from a needle or punch or a fall
but a slicing, tender-sting touch or word.

Today I am in a ball so it must be bad,
I cannot look at anything or anyone full on,
if I am lucky I will be left to rest as I am,
escape, of course, always in my mind.
The leaves bank up outside confused by gusts and feet
relapsing into heaps.
No-one comes to pay, again, so I stay put.

The Way It Goes
Mother/Daughter

It winds and dips as song and stories should
from the tap tap of her tiny foot
and she asks again 'Do squirrels eat baddies?'
and because I can I say 'Yes'
so she will be pleased.

Evensong

The end of our last day.
Light spun just for us on the hill above.
Gold flecks. Gold Dust. Already how magicked we feel,
watched over by the disused windmill,
a benevolent giant in transition from a working life
to one of pleasure and contemplation, sail-less but hopeful.
I swing her from the caravan door into her first pair of Wellingtons.
Four slices of dying bread in a Safeway bag.
Treasure.

The fields to the first gate are fat with water and swallow us whole.
I stroke and hold her hand at the same time.
We pass older families having a knock-about on the tennis court
and another mother snags me a knowing, tender gaze.

To the stile smeared with the blood of South Devon mud,
the feet that have gone before us.
I lift her over. She waits, balanced on the thin beam
as I pull myself over and just before we rejoin hands
and I draw her to safety, I imagine, as I have since her birth, a fall,
or worse, disaster ever close, threatening to take her.

Deeper into wild meadow, words wait for her,
the start of names; *daisy, buttercup, cow parsley.*
A vapour in the air.
A shimmer shake mist-veil.
What that mummy?
The chase for detail but for now I savour her own explanations.
She cannot see the moon so she tells me it is hiding.

At the first lake we talk about our visit to Paignton Zoo,
especially the lions.
She makes the roar and in the dip of sun, the near-dark rinse,
it seems all fantastical creatures are upon us,
rising out from the runnels of ploughed earth.

The ducks are all hiding too or else we are
blinded by the thick stages of green;
wafers of lily pads, bloated finger reeds
and the upside-down sky eaten by planes of waters.
<u>Back home</u> we would be unaware of these slow changes in light,
being indoors and well-lit.

She looks up at me in wonder to say *it's comin'*
excited about the dark and it is all before us.

At the second lake, still no ducks,
the air peppered with midges,
earth and sky blending,
scenes momentarily set in aspic,
ferns assisting the overall design.
A conjured stillness suspends purpose.
Birch and rowan neck closer.
Our legs are bloodied.
We find a dead frog and she sings a good song about frogs,
she does not understand it is dead just *sleepin'*, makes a sad face.
Later, on the way back, she knows where to find it again
and wants to pick it up and give it a cuddle.

We can still hear them playing tennis
as we get to an old, splintered sign of burnt letters: LAKE WALK
and open the old five-bar gate into a denser place.
Interior.
Under the arch of cat's cradle branches,
she skips away through the undergrowth desperate to hold her,
briars, tangleweed, ivy, nettles and dock leaves like mothers near by.
She picks a dandelion, crushes it and suddenly wants to
go back to Grandma minding her baby sister.

I don't want the walk to end but we retrace our steps
from the spools of smaller lakes and waterlogged paths,
footprints evaporating.
A cooler air and sunset crush us together.

The lichen on the trees is too beautiful,
laced ceramics, iced and fragile,
barely holding on, but at the same time clinging,
and I show her and she pokes and breaks some,
then repeats the word and laughs.

Two Canada geese appear on the first lake,
swim knowingly towards us and we give up the treasure,
redirect an inky language before it can be translated.
My turn. My turn.

Returning over the stile,
my own mother, holding the baby, another girl,
waves out into the gloom from the caravan window.
My first born runs off, leaving the lakes, the lichen, the dead frog
and me with the image of her running through to a perfect dissolve
and my own breath, loud and visible,
reminding me that I am very, very cold.

Notes on Mapreading

'Conventional signs are used where there is no room on paper to show the true outline, or to add a written description . . . For ease of recognition, conventional signs are as suggestive of the object represented as possible. Thus the sign for a windmill could scarcely be mistaken for anything else.'
    (*Notes on Mapreading*, The War Office, 1929, Reprinted with Amendments, 1939)

Don't touch me. Again. Felt.
New husbands appear in every crowd scene.
Relearning this way of moving
and how to use my eyes.
How long exactly were we together?

Cutting me up on the inside lane.
Nothing personal.

I think our friendship has slipped away
with the pretence of not noticing.
It has to be over, now.
Please, please stop popping round for coffee.

Lost notebooks bother me at nights.

Big, big skies and vast rolls of cloud over the col
(and we know we both love days like these).
But nothing is really clear.
At the kissing gate. Unsure.

Hold me.
Stop me from phoning you.
Don't.

Col: a neck or ridge of land connecting two mountains or hills. A col is lower than the mountains or hills it connects, and higher than the surrounding plain or valleys.

Glass Blower

Half way down the pier,
between the amusement arcade
and the speedboat rides,
all weathers,
in or out of season,
the glass blower is teasing
out delicate, blue legs
the colour of Indian ocean shallows
feathered with a discoed sunlight,
waiting to be attached to bodies of deer,
still unmade but resting in abstraction.

His finished creatures are optimistic:
dazzling butterflies, starry-eyed kittens
and a favourite with the Saga crowd
and foreign students, cupid puppies,
each one ready to travel the world.
They shimmer with
the promise of the bright lights
of a bedside cabinet and a lingering polish.

From their show-height the glass animals look out
above the slurry of brown shingle and
a thick, grey English Channel
to a clear point on the horizon.
They never see the chipped and shattered,
abandoned and mutant,
that get reheated into a perfect sunset
that might recreate a foal to frolic
across a mantelpiece.

He wraps each baby in a blanket of cerise tissue,
seals them with a jealous but tender smile,
the Daddy he never was and sometimes
he lets the glass go its own way,
shuts up shop early and waits,
heart pumping in the Gents
for the shape of a stranger.

Sitter

It is a discrete corner
Where her days pass
Below 'T' on the Fiction shelves
And today in the warm library
Life and written life try to hold her interest
But nothing captures her soul
Turns the slow face to turn
The quiet heart to speed
Like the flood of rain pouring through the high window
And the librarian's frantic rush to seal it.

Remembering Songs (Instrumental)

Let us take that walk to the sea, by
the turns and the tricks in the paving
and the bricks, to the land's edge, the
water's start, three generations we,
mothers and mothers before us and

mothers more to be; whispers, secrets,
indifferences, muted by the lip-seal of
moss, ornamental and wild, sucking at
our heels. Late afternoon, early evening,
passed the sleight-of-hand front gardens,

small hotels: *Seaforth, Oakholme, Silverdale,*
with their dressing-ups (and downs),
hang-dog vacancies swinging between
scowl and grin and the converted
Victorian flats keeping steady their

watch behind long, velveteen lashes to
the path, the tread and sway of our legs,
out-of-kilter metronomes beating time
away. From thresholds, doors held ajar,
to let the air in, and small crimes out,

a caught breath, after barren months
and the blather of cold winds, the
buntings out and flashing about, fat
and full to bursting, the cherry trees,
breaking their backs, exhausted but

happy, pretty May Queens waving us
by, nearly there, to the corner, the view,
the end of the day, the chase and the
bloom, waiting beyond us. Already
at our feet blossom has fallen, some

spoiled and torn, beginnings of words,
the looks we shared and missed. Above
still the unbroken hold fast until a
glancing kiss nudges a flower to fall
and miscarried a single petal floats free,

a slither-pinked whisk and whip of
such beauty and promise, we remember
again the moment of birth, given and
made. Every journey has its rest, the
petal lands, unsettles the freshly raked

patterns on the gravel, the order of the
Japanese formal garden and the English
suburban drive. My daughter loosens
her hand from mine and skips ahead,
leaves a still hot keepsake where the curl

of her matched my own, a thread of
dying sun stealing over the slates and
hard edges blurs her to a smudge as she
dance-kicks a fury of blossom that snags
the light, moves itself again, reaches out

from the railings and box hedges, reverses
and mowings, *flower, flower, mummy,* in
the say the fixing, ikedori, teaching the
right word, my mother reins back her
hand and they go on together, smiling

and complete. In arriving, already we
know where we are going, between the
words still to come and the ones we have
lost, between the blossom above and the
petals on the ground. Early evening, late

afternoon, to the shore line, tears quick to
dry and to hide in the sea's spray, behind
the ranks of cherry trees endure, having
seen it all before passing on and through,
tomorrow I will tell her Daddy has gone.

Ikedori: Japanese garden-design concept meaning 'capturing alive'.

The Pictorial Encyclopaedia of Fishes

Seen on Live Cam, at four minute intervals,
Photographs of Niagara Falls
People looking beyond people seen static
While waters move in instances of watching
Moving stills moving still.

Mine

watch you   take hold   of you   that means me
    in a mirror
        the name   the place   her   your
my world   held scratch tight hit held until   near broken
                                    and done
        left for another   to claim   lost and smashed
        my world   my moon   hiding in the day
    my smile and lick   my baby sister   loving her   me
your plucked eye
    me
            all mine

Long Rock

Long shot of a lean landed, dust balled place of industrial estates and tooth-grinning terraces backing onto train tracks, overhead lines and the Channel desperate for the Atlantic to make it. Outskirts. One road. Mini-roundabouts. The dangerous level crossing is where I miss my lover who has just shot through while I wait for the sleeper out from Penzance to riddle by on its metal haunches. I feel like Meryl Streep in that awful but watchable commuters-fall-in-love film, you know the one, where she thinks she's blown it with Robert De Niro. The wind is up and the kite surfers stunting it close to St Michael's Mount. Something famous is lurking in the wings behind Davey & Gilbert's electrical showrooms. Fade to the other Long Rock where extras are waiting for make-up in chalets 4-10, the salvage yard turns casino, cranes make it snow, John, at Plumb Base, triumphs, cast as the unknown lead in a drugs caper and zombies drive killer trucks in and out. I, however, am looking for outdoor lighting, lost between the frozen fish packers and a unit selling grommets. When I drive round for the second time and check locations on the map, I notice someone following me in a blue sedan. I test his nerve, squeal into reverse. We chase from Mexico Inn to Safeway where he shoots passed to Marazion, becomes just another dog-walker marching up the sands, well-lit, half-scripted, imagining his big moment when he will take me out. I dump the car, walk into the waves. End shot. No-one is quite sure. But on a good note the new director at Kwik-Fit thinks he can get Marisa Tomei to do a cameo. Later, some time in the night there is an unexplained explosion at K & R's timber yard. *Cut to the suddenly silent crowd.*

Last sentence from the script for the film 'Bicycle Thieves' by Vittorio De Sica.

Stitchery

'It is possible to change almost any material or article from the ordinary and commonplace to something of interest and beauty by the addition of few or many stitches.'
(Margaret Munro, *The Big Book of Needlecraft*)

Half sisters, we meet for the first time in *Patisserie Valerie*
half way down Marylebone High Street.
At thirty-five I am the older by two years.
I recognise her immediately,
sitting in the centre of the café facing the door,
she has his eyes and colouring.
Unplanned we embrace and both tear up,
order quickly: a pot of English Breakfast and a plate of shortbread.
Talk comes fast over the long years apart,
mostly we check notes on having the same father and settle some mysteries.
I let her know that I missed the funeral because no-one had told me he died.
She had, naturally, wanted to know why.
I sense everyone is listening in and I don't blame them.
We take a necessary pause before rushing on, finding much to share;
a childhood with single mothers in south-coast seaside towns,
falling in love at seventeen and still with the same partners,
choosing humanities at degree and working in the same industry,
living just one postcode away from each other for ten years.
We do well to hold it together, to keep the big tears away.
Three hours and ten minutes.
I like her. We will meet again. We make that promise.
A parting embrace. A kiss that makes it all better, now.
I think of my own young daughters,
cuddled up together in the same bed some nights
and as I walk away of course I think of what might have been
but feel renewed, no longer only child,
better late than never.
I fold the happy thought of her deep down inside me,
can just about stop myself shouting out loud
I have a sister. I really have.

Bench

'For who can bear to be forgotten'
        (David Bowie, *Richochet*)

I am still new, caught up in the near thrill of where
I find myself, at the hub, the rib and rinse, the metal
and meat of a fast-fast city that whips about me,
happening just there beyond the no statues shush of
Brunswick Square Gardens, a less important cousin

to Russell Square (although we are both WC1) with
its fat formal beds and busy café, who in turn knows
its place beneath the grand ol' daddy Hyde Park,
somewhere I hear tell from tired tourists, before
they roll back to the gaggle-clutch of hotels that huddle

round Euston and Kings Cross (I like the sound of
the names, it shows I know them, that I am not just
sitting here doing nothing). I have no memory of when
I came here, it seems I have always been the third
bench to the right, forming a loose but crooked smile

with my identical neighbours. We keep ourselves to
ourselves aside from essential weather comments and
the odd disaster (the death of Joe a quiet, loveable
drunk last winter or the arrest of four teenagers
smoking dope just yesterday), incidents draw us close,

nearly move us. I am a full stop to the babble, the
dance and cut of getting on with purpose, I let you
stay a while, loll, lose time and wait, sometimes make
important decisions and leave to take a different way
from the time before you sat down, such moments

make me proud. But mostly I just am, you come with
your drink, drugs, fights, farts, kisses, shopping and
stories from the world around the corner, the wind's
talk in the dry holly tree, just out of my reach, past
the brow of the fence, the sigh of the oaks, fragments

of blurred litter, the hiss-smack of a tennis ball hitting
me in the back again, and the tantalising swing-squeal
of the gate, ever ajar, smirking with a secret knowledge;
how a couple broke up after watching *Last Tango in
Paris* from the Bertolucci season at the Renoir (I can just

see the billboard), and further out of sight to the British
Museum where things have taken a place in history and
cabinets, then down to the thread of the Thames, the view
from Hungerford Bridge, marking out a mantra of famous
sights, the way the light . . . and then I am nothing, blind

soundless frets of wood, empty municipal bones,
dreaming of what might be, no inscription, replaceable,
frightened of grafitti and growing old in a space that
may be no more than a damp corner of balding grass
and dog shit, where you are always only passing by me.

'from the world around the corner, the wind's talk in the dry holly tree'
is from T S Eliot's *The Family Reunion*.

Shine

Taken from dreaming
not really waking but sleeping
mist again
pulls her eyes into the slow field
where unnamed undergrowth completes her.

At the window
where she lays her head
children are throwing stones
but she cannot hear them.
She forgets whether she has two or three of her own
and cannot tell whether they are laughing or dying
but the sky is holding them up
so they might be angels.

Some mornings it seems everything needs cleaning
again and again and again
and after cleaning
measuring
the way the forks sit in the cutlery drawer
the way the clothes hang between one another
and other ways that she has not yet invented
until the hour loops round with more dirt and worry and
stray dogs, called family, near her door.

She lives by water now
and has a view
most would call beautiful
but she only sees tangles coming in from the sides
breaking her line.

He comes home with freesias
and she puts them in a vase
thinking about murder and suicide
as she arranges their imperfect stems.

At night, folded and alert,
she sees hairs on freshly washed pillows and listens out
for the movement of dust in the hall.
He sleeps, beside her, inaccurately.

In the dark the same old song,
the table is laid
each place set
and her life has not even begun yet.

Stones at Dunster

'The dead are always present'
    (Kanakakis, *Cretan Artist*)

This is the day
Cold but clear
I want to have hold me as I die
When we walked on Dunster beach
And felt quiet amazement at the stones
As if conceived and crafted
Yet in the same instance perfect in themselves
Just stones
Stones by sea by sky.

We found the one
It had polish and comfort
A happy, weighted stone
And we took it back to accompany us at home.

He, if I go before him,
Will pick me out and carry me off
But chances are I will be lost underfoot
Get washed back and covered over by the crowds
And he will be left alone
Until he cannot remember
How I was
We were
We did
And forgets me
Just as easily as that day
Might have turned out dull
And after throwing a few stones into the waves
We headed back
Wondering why we had bothered to go there.

Myrrh

Because it was, after all, not special enough, we
played out the last shout into a useless night up on its
hinges, stitched up and dog-wacked. In the lounge
stupid cowboys waiting for the other to make a move.

The Founded Heart

Barbara Hepworth's House and Garden, St Ives, Summer 2002

You are not here today but beyond us
the gulls are smashing up the sky
gravel paths are bothered with visitors
fresh from the exhibits
letters in your own hand talking of
Mondrian, Dali, Picasso 'what a sweetie',
enormous black and white photographs in cases
from young girl to old woman
all beautifully installed and catalogued.

The studio is as you left it
a row of dirty coats hanging on their hooks
folds of skincloth
too too perfect to be casual.
We come perhaps with a disposition for the
arrangement.

Each fat curve and every polished touching
imprints on the present
reminds and shapes us knowingly and abstractly
whether we have stumbled upon you
or made a special time to visit and written it down.

In the garden your plants have been curated:
myrtle, laurel, nile lily, escallonia
words that cannot bend.
Here, in a corner the unmentioned dry shards of bamboo.
The sculptures grow bigger beside them.
Wood
      Metal   Stone

The space between remains our desire.

Explaining Mary

Twin girls
identical
in navy, velvet coats
and best T-bar patent black shoes
stare up at an idol of Mary
in Lucena's *San Martin* church.
Daddy tells Mary's story
and they listen with fat eyes.
A priest coughs in the confessional
some tourists shunter passed
seeking out the famed baroque detailing
in the *sagrario* chapel
and the twins begin to suck
on delicate entrails of red liquorice
bleeding in the evening gloom
waiting to bite with their
sharp, little teeth.

Lucena is in Córdoba province, Andalucia.

Holiday Romance
A True Story

The heat is in her just seventeen-year-old body, wails from a nearby minaret remind her she is in Tunisia. The hotel complex is vast and white and clean. She paddles and floats, settles into shade, takes sun in seconds, drinks a version of Fanta. She went on an excursion that ended with the set where they shot the first Star Wars film and a camel ride with an older woman, on holiday alone,

on the fringes of the desert, the Sahara, snapped behind them as they smiled for a photograph from her parents coupled on a mirror camel, spitting and rolling its eyes. At night she leaves dinner early and goes to the club where she has met a boy who wants to have sex with her, but she is only there for a week so she keeps him at bay, dates some others, goes back to him, visits his cousin's house

in Sousse, meets his friends. He is half French and half Tunisian, with dreadlocks, his name is Zou Zou. She finds him beautiful. But she won't fuck him. On her last night she goes back with him and his friends to the house where she went before and at midnight a man arrives and takes a shine to her. He calls himself Frankenstein, he shows her scars all over his body, she decides

to go back to her hotel, but he won't let her and Zou Zou is cowering in the hallway, his friends playing cards nervously in the bedroom. She gets up to go, Frankenstein pulls her back, eats some glass, cuts himself. Of course she screams and that is what he wants, he laughs and cuts himself some more and says in broken English 'You, understand'. For the first time she is cold, she tries

to play cards with him and some of the others, one boy is crying in a corner, she smiles, keeps quiet, calm, then, when he is caught up in the game with Zou Zou she goes to creep out. He sees her, grabs her, takes her into the back room, one high window, locks the door, takes out a knife. 'You understand.' And she believes her life is over, but stays smiling, saying anything to get out of the locked room and wondering what Zou Zou and his friends are doing, knowing they are too frightened to do anything. He motions for her to lie down. Then the knock comes. She recognises the voice, Zou Zou's cousin, a girl, talking fast in Arabic, Frankenstein opens the door a crack, she thrusts her hand through, mouths 'Help', the girl seems to be fighting her corner, telling him off, she

knows he could cut her at any moment. She holds the cousin's hand, Frankenstein grips her shoulder, waves the knife, somehow they get into the hall, the cousin still arguing and then into the alley. She sees Zou Zou and his friends sitting in the dust, head in hands, shaking, his best friend Olivier says 'I'm so sorry'. Frankenstein starts to get angry with the cousin, he loosens his

hold on her, Zou Zou beckons her to run, she does, she runs and runs and tries to remember where to go, down to the beach, it is late, early, maybe 3 am, she doesn't look back, there is some shouting behind her. She feels every beat of her heart, runs inside a hotel, into a room where a man is typing, it is surreal, he looks up, she shouts for him to lock the door and he doesn't speak English but

gets the idea, locks the door, she falls in his arms and he enjoys touching her up, but she doesn't care because he doesn't have a knife. Minutes later Zou Zou and the boys run to the hotel, she lets them in, they fall at her feet. She finds out they knew him, that he had been in prison for murder. Then she understands. Zou Zou had just wanted to scare her, to get her back for not sleeping with him

and it had all gone horribly wrong. He tells her Frankenstein wanted to rape her, kill her, kill them and kill himself. She leaves in a taxi. No police. Dust in every crease of her body. She creeps into bed in the room next to her parents. She flies home the next day, tells no-one, watches the sun set over the burnt clouds, feels lucky, will never stop telling herself that it really happened.

Bridge/Water

We stand on the wooden bridge above a stream
My one-year-old daughter and I
She watches the way of the water
From there
To there
From there
To there
Leaning over to catch it
Disappearing under the bridge
Wondering how it moves
From one side to another
But is still there again
Back where it started.

Graded Pieces

when a world is just over there
threads hanging in a mudded afternoon
it is not plain or viable to do anything
beyond remaining taut
trying to place a field above another
find a position from which to judge the moment
and oneself

the emphasis is on tuning and tempo
levels of difficulty
expression tantamount to a breath of life

the examination room is large
oak panelled
and naturally cold
tall, svelte windows offer slices
of a thick matted garden beyond
where rhododendrons appear rich and rare
but outrun all other species

the entrance into the room
remains the same from this day onwards
the footfalls on the parquet floor
the observations
the instrument to the neck
beginning with confidence or . . .

certificates might hang on walls or remain in drawers
now I like to think I play for myself
but mostly I lie
thinking I have escaped the fret and feel
of a best performance

Picnic

after seeing Fernand Leger's 'La Partie de Campagne' (final version), 1954,
oil on canvas, Maeght Foundation, Saint Paul, French Riviera, May 2003

We amaze ourselves, outside
amongst the lower slopes of beautiful pines
that bend in ways we admire,
on stolen and found blankets
we are arranged so
sky adhering to mostly bare shoulders so
illuminated by a saturation of late afternoon sun
compelling
although someone and perhaps something is clearly
missing from the grouping,
(birds of an unknown species alight, bears – the small,
brown kind found in these parts or so we are told – hide)
and we know we only have a certain amount of time left
before shadows stop being interesting
and the curl in the path beckons a slow climb down
to the destinations where we will disperse
and try to remember who and what was there,
as if we were playing the tray game at a child's party,
definite about the elegant slice of a woman
who caught all our attention,
missing children in her eyes,
and a man without a soul
picking at grass and saying little,
otherwise a few bread crumbs,
a greasy knife waiting to be washed,
a near touch
violets
laughter
an unsure perspective,
colour all gone.

Scenes in an Afternoon

Sssh! Quiet on Set!
Don't blame the challenge of deceit
nor anything else
these things are just here again in a row
for what they are nothing more –
the ridge of birch trees crooning a score
low slung avenues humming intent
disappointing movements of badly lit bones
you talking about doing something this evening
a lorry bleating its reversal
and a forest path mapped out for the useless
a highlighted lake
just three miles from an underpass
the possible importance of a flask
an A road
fields
motorists
a sighting of butcher-birds
a shooting gallery
wondering when they will kiss
conforming to a genre
CUT!
unfinished

Pin

Unstable, then, I was put away for a while, unspecified low-rise
mental hospital by chalk-scuffed fields. I shared a room with Linda.
When I arrived she wasn't there, the nurse was casual in her explanation,
she was having ECT treatment. Only tamazipan for me thank God
but at the time I would have happily let them go and wire me up.
In the day-room, pretty bleak, near pointless puzzles and ping-pong,
a mix of schizos, divorcees, manic depressives, suicides and unspecific
illnesses like my own. In occupational therapy we painted mostly and
some sewed, that must have been where Linda got the pin. On my
second night in I heard the steady scratching. I sat up in bed and peered
across at Linda in the half light hunched over and working away
at a steady pace on her wrist. She must have known I could see her but
she didn't care or stop. I sped down the corridor to get the night staff who
were playing Trivial Pursuits. They were unsurprised and reluctant to
leave the game. (It was an entertainment question, something about
Marilyn Monroe.) I guess they knew there was no hurry with a pin.
When they got to Linda she gave up willingly, no fight. She had just
sheered off a few skin layers and left the faintest smudge of blood on
 her sheets. One nurse told me the week before it had been a biro.
They took her away to sleep in restraints. The next morning at breakfast,
her wrist bandaged, she sat down to a boiled egg and cut her toast into
soldiers. I noticed that she left the knife safely on the table. They brought
her back to my room two nights later wearing only a slim plaster.
She seemed quiet but calm. I asked her if she was fine. A quick nod.
I worried about my possessions and their potential: face flannel, nail file,
toothbrush, mascara, paper. But she went straight to sleep. The next day
she began the 1000 piece puzzle of Leeds Castle. I left two weeks later.
Linda was still there. I often wonder if she found the right way in the end.

Half an Hour

Tonight, tonight the same streets are breeding a shift
into a lesser known place that makes me doubt the
way to the Golden Chip Shop on Farringdon Road.

In half an hour I am sunk by the glut of fierce eyes,
hungry for blood, a suck, a steal; menace everywhere
in the familiar dips and turns. I slip into someone

I no longer resemble. I might not make it back
to the family waiting for their one large cod with chips,
no vinegar, two plaice, one battered sausage. Already

I am imagining the person I will become, out the loop,
where all that is left of me is the mutilated evidence
of a fish supper squalling in a gutter close to home.

Two Weeks

We will undo ourselves
by the time we arrive back
but appear to be similar
tanned perhaps
shouldering an experience
to dent the surface,
the rephrased story from a photograph
where the real journey went beyond
the path from the Temple of Isis behind olive
bushes where smiles transgressed, scorched
and exhausted by their own derivative grin.
But, already, the familiar roads home have us,
news is twenty-four hour,
work the next morning claims us
and as we are talking about
the holiday it already sounds wrong
and the listeners are not really listening
to the details between the details
just imagining a smart double room with sea view
a hot sun
pearlised
down to the free soap
which we saved and brought back
still born, perfect wrapped
ready for our guests to use
the real evidence gone with the chambermaid
a new body laying out their toiletries
in the bathroom in a country where marble is cheap.

Gatherers

Easter Egg Hunt, Lauderdale House, Highgate

I am not here, again. But I appear to myself, today as
mother hen, I spread the picnic blanket out for the friends
and their children to join my own for the *eggstravaganza*.
(Egg hunts being something I might have thought I wanted
as a child.) Already, on arriving, one child is out, sicking
up avocado, the others running wild with the rest, and we
are hunkering down into staying with, minding buggies,
queuing for tickets. Back in our packs we make eggs for
rolling later from torn up newspaper inside Safeway bags,
decorate the sides with scraps of wrapping paper. Pecking

magpies one and all, on the grab for the shiny, a bit of glitz
on a morning shedding a weak sun. Parents eye each other's
groupings for sellotape, which being in demand, has made
for murderous intent; for the element of competition, the
best egg, the fastest roller, has spurred us on beyond the
usual *my child is better, prettier, look at them*, horrors that
contain us into near touching that inevitably turns to
shoving to force the activity, the day into being special,
parents scrambling to make their children, all knitted
together, stand out. I sense already the best of it has been

had in the planning, becalmed rooms with Earl Grey that did
not get knocked over or need to be placed out of reach,
afternoons when a sun lit them splendidly in the Georgian
withdrawing room. In practice the egg hunt is already
scuppered (of course it always would be) by older ones who
have gone round snatching up the white tickets which could
be exchanged for cream eggs. We drag up the hill for the
rolling with snarls and moans from the children, then more
tears, as irregular eggs dislodge, fail, while the few winners
punch victory salutes at a sky spitting a steadfast drizzle.

Kissing Gourami

Her boy in spiderman T-shirt lags behind the buggy
she steers ruthlessly. The chisel of her face is bitten
spare and keen, an element of foul weather about
the look,

the no touch, keep off my fucking patch stare. Her
voice is a sling-shot. A boy and a girl, no more
now, nor then but for Him now soon to be
gone,

for all her giving, bringing up, keeping house,
staying up late for his late comings, his big job,
she was (still is) proud of Him, for Him, fuck him,
he's done them down.

When her kids are on the swings the other
mothers wait longer than they might want to,
the park is hers for the taking if she wants it, and
she hates it

having to go there every day, not wanting to go
home only keeping her going back. She leans
against the slide, watches her little man dance
in a puddle

getting wet to the skin while her toddler girl eats
sand and grins hard. A small sigh. She leaves
them spooling in a brief magic. Blows them a rare
kiss.

The name Kissing Gourami derives from the fact that these fishes have a habit of pressing their thick-lipped mouths together as if they are kissing. In fact, however, these appear to be quarrels between rivals. In Indonesia it is valued as a food fish.

Hedgerow

Yesterday we spoke out beyond ourselves,
because we were almost forgotten
and they thought they could just take things away.
Around us headline clouds glanced over.
Our bones rooted us down
with stone and stipple and web and waft,
as beings next to another and another still.

That night the distilled beauty of a sunset over a polished sea
demanded attention;
stopped
a mother from her child to look from the window,
a farmer from his evening path,
a car of strangers to park up,
and there, the hedgerow,
around the barbs and softer leaves,
a found language,
making its part, directing the eye,
chasing thought into an action of there,
seeing and being in on the count.

A day later the granite reclaimed everything,
tracked with the making and doing
of more ages than our brief conceit.

The demonstration of white bluebells lasted most of May
at the sides of the roads then folded.
Heather started its march over the moors.
The air ambulance found another dead climber.
A horizon stayed unsure.

In 2002 local people in and around West Penwith held the largest protest rally ever staged in Cornwall against the closing of their local A&E hospital in Penzance and overturned the immediate decision to initiate a closure.

Lobby

'There are some places I ain't never really been.'
*(Overheard conversation, No 7 bus, Paddington to British Museum,
just passing Selfridges, Oxford Street, afternoon, September 2002)*

The hotel holds me in its own arms
those wide spun landing pads
thick seated sofas and light chinking sounds
coming to a stop at eager angles
and angels at reception desks.
A key card is a precious artefact.
The mirrors in the lift make half my face disappear.
The other world beyond the bedroom door
is a place where towels keep arriving.

The decision is slate. Delabole. Expensive.
To make an entrance set off the rest of the house.

I have taken a number
and hold it, fold it, ball it,
seal it to my inner palm
secret and almost forgotten
until the click and call
of the fallen moment
going in to find out if I am still
alive after all
or want ten slices of luncheon
meat with a smiling face inside.

At Trieste all trains are downed by snow
breaking records for the winter of '85
and I am going nowhere but the station.
Forty years before me, my grandfather
came here at the end of the war,
rested a while then passed on.

I am cargo
flicking through old magazines
in a language I don't understand
wearing all my clothes and still feeling cold.

Hush!
Someone is coming towards me.
I get to my feet.
Feeling real enough.
The waiting is over
and I shimmy through
to a single pixel.